THE NATURE OF GHOSTS

PRAISE FOR THE WORK OF BREANNAN MATRIS

"I am an employee of The St. John's Cinema in Portland, Oregon. Breannan sensed a ghost in the theater and talked to us about doing an investigation. We agreed to this and were actually present for much of it. Breannan and the team of investigators collected clear evidence of a "presence," primarily through audio recording. Due to the fact that I was present for this taping, I'm certain that the voice was not from any team members present. Breannan later did a clearing ritual and since that time (nine months) we have not heard or felt anything from our strange visitor. I found Breannan's abilities to be exceptional as she demonstrated skill and psychic sensitivity in an easygoing, discreet, and professional manner. I would highly recommend her for finding and sending any lost souls that need a nudge."

—Donna P. L., Gearhart, OR

"I have written several books on folklore and the paranormal. As part of my work, over the past twelve years I have conducted many paranormal investigations of my own. During the two years I have known Breannan, we have visited several locations together that had a reputation for paranormal events. In that time, Breannan consistently demonstrated an extraordinary sense of intuition. On several occasions, we visited places she knew very little about because I purposely withheld the facts and historic information about the locale. She voiced impressions of past residents and events in the locales that were too detailed and consistently correct to have been a series of 'lucky guesses.'"

—Jefferson Davis, Vancouver, WA

"Breannan assisted me in ridding a ghost from my home. I lived with the ghost for about a year, but he had become threatening and I no longer felt safe there. Breannan was able to give details about the ghost that I could confirm, including his name and how he died. She also told me that I would have a dream that evening that would be an important message from this entity. Not only did I have a dream as she said, but the entity gave me information that Breannan had shared with him that I had no way of knowing. It has been five months now and my home has been peaceful. I'm thankful there are people like Breannan in the world and am grateful for her services."

—"Beth" B., Oregon City, OR

"My mother's home became haunted and it got to the point she could not spend more than fifteen minutes in the home without feeling ill. The home was left vacant for five years because of this. My mother did not believe in the paranormal and had her doubts about a house clearing, but she had exhausted all other options. Following Breannan's clearing, my mother said she couldn't ignore the feeling of this new energy in the home. She became 'a believer' after the clearing and returned home and fell in love with her house all over again."

— MJ Hopkins, Springfield, OR

The Nature of Ghosts

Who They Are, What They Are,
and Why They're Here

BREANNAN S. MATRIS

LUMINARE PRESS
WWW.LUMINAREPRESS.COM

The Nature of Ghosts: Who They Are, What They Are
and Why They're Here
Copyright © 2024 by Breannan S. Matris

All rights reserved. This book or any portion thereof may not be
reproduced or used in any manner whatsoever without the express
written permission of the publisher, except for the use of brief
quotations in a book review.

Printed in the United States of America

Luminare Press
442 Charnelton St.
Eugene, OR 97401
www.luminarepress.com

LCCN: 2024901556
ISBN: 979-8-88679-485-4

This book is dedicated to my late father, Jim, who was a tough skeptic on all matters pertaining to the spirit, but now, most assuredly, has seen the light.

TABLE OF CONTENTS

Foreword 3
Introduction 5

1. History of Belief in Ghosts 7
2. My Encounters with Ghosts 11
3. Who They Are 18
4. Becoming a Ghost 23
5. Alfred—A Ghost of Passion 27
6. Steve—A Fear-Based Ghost 30
7. Ben—A Ghost in Confusion 33
8. What Ghosts Are 36
9. Ghosts Versus Spirits 40
10. Why We Fear Ghosts 43
11. Why They Haunt 46
12. Why They Remain 48
13. Completing the Transition 51

Selected Resources 53
Bibliography 55
Notes 57
About the Author 61

"Quantum physics has taught us that, in the final analysis, everything is energy."[1]

—JOHN KACHUBA,
The Missing Peace in Your Life

FOREWORD

For over twenty years, I have researched and written about the paranormal, particularly in the Pacific Northwest. Because I am not psychic, as part of my research I often gather the insights of a paranormal consultant—commonly called a psychic—on field visits. I do not share any information with them before the visit. Instead, I ask them for their impressions of the property we visit, which I compare with my historic research and witness interviews.

Over the years, many people who sincerely believe they have some kind of extrasensory gift have approached me, asking to participate in my research. Many of them do have a gift, but few stand out for the high percentage of their impressions that tally with the facts surrounding my investigations.

I met Breannan several years ago and worked with her on many investigations. I believe she is one of those highly gifted individuals with insight into the paranormal forces existing in the background of our everyday world. She voiced impressions of past residents or events in the locales that were detailed and consistently correct. In addition to her ability to gather facts on paranormal events in haunted locations, Breannan has demonstrated her ability to clear unpleasant spiritual forces, much to the relief of several property owners.

Over the years, I suggested that Breannan write a book detailing her work. When she asked me to write the foreword to this volume, which is her first book, I was pleased, honored, and humbled to do so. I hope you, the reader, will be as impressed with Breannan's research into the paranormal and her gifts as I am.

—Jefferson Davis,
author of *Weird Washington*
and *Weird Oregon*

INTRODUCTION

I am a psychic medium who grew up in a haunted house. I became aware of the existence of ghosts at a very early age. As an adult, I joined several ghost hunting groups in an effort to learn more about them. During this process I grew to feel compassion, not only for the people living among ghosts, but for ghosts themselves, and I became determined to help both the living and the ghosts in their home. I embarked on the study of the nature of ghosts and developed a practice of clearing. By assisting them in moving from their current environment and into their natural home, I believe I helped bring peace to both the living and the ghosts with whom they lived.

In order to develop an effective practice, I realized I had to first explore the nature of ghosts. I sought answers to such questions as who they are, what they are, why they remain earthbound, what their needs and capabilities are, whether they pose a danger to us, and how to best communicate with them, to name a few. After gaining insight into their natures I began sharing this information by giving talks on the radio and on podcasts, speaking at ghost conferences, and participating in ghost tours. Following these presentations, many would ask me if I had written on the subject of ghosts. It is in response to this inquiry that I have written *The Nature of Ghosts: Who They Are, What They Are, and Why They're Here*. In the following chapters, I will discuss my interactions with ghosts, how they come to be, what they are constructed of, what they are capable of, and if they should be feared. I'm looking forward to creating my next book, which will focus on how to clear them.

—Breannan Matris

1

History of Belief in Ghosts

*"A man should look for what is,
and not what he thinks should be."*[2]

—Albert Einstein

Ghosts are ancient and have walked among us for many thousands of years. Doctor Irving Hinkle writes in his first book, *The First Ghosts*, that evidence of this can be seen in cuneiform (or clay) tablets dating back as far as 3000 BC depicting ghostly figures as well as writings about them[3]. These tablets were found in what is now the Middle East, revealing depictions of ghosts as well as instructions on how to deal with them. Anthropologists have suggested these were attempts to communicate that something of a person survives after death. Early literature, including religious passages, makes mention of ghosts, and tales of ghost encounters have thrived throughout the centuries. One of the earliest known published ghost stories is from the first century AD; a famous attorney, Gaius Caecilius, (otherwise known as Pliny the Younger), wrote about his experiences with an old, bearded man who haunted his farmhouse.[4] Further, every culture throughout history has, at some point, created ritual practices for dealing with ghosts.

Despite ghosts being depicted in art, literature, and cultural practices throughout human history, belief in ghosts has fluctuated throughout time. As the United States approached the nineteenth century, for example, rapid advances in science seemed to disprove the existence of ghosts. These scientific advancements ultimately created a rise in materialism, or the notion that all that exists is physical matter in a panoply of variations. Materialism then overshadowed spiritualism and the belief in the existence of ghosts.

Dr. Robert Watson, an American scientist and early advocate of materialism, set the stage for this decrease in the belief in ghosts when he proclaimed that science has "rooted out every theory that involved such relics of…superstition as mind, consciousness, or soul [or spirit]." Further, since no one had ever touched or seen a soul (or spirit) in a test tube, and because "what cannot be touched or seen eludes objective verification," then "it must be dismissed as nonexistent."[5] Dr. Watson's proclamations became widely popular in The United States around the turn of the twentieth century and as a result, ghosts came to be largely dismissed as fantasy.[6]

Not until 1848 was the reality of ghosts once again opened for debate. Two young farm girls, Catherine (Kate) and Margaretta (Maggie) Fox, who lived just outside Rochester, New York are largely responsible for the revitalization of spiritualism. The Fox sisters became celebrities after exposing what appeared to be ghostly activity in their home. As children, Kate and Maggie would hear loud tapping sounds from within the walls of their farmhouse. Over time, they discovered this tapping was not random but rather in response to events in their home. The girls then developed a system whereby they would ask a question and a "yes" answer would be indicated by two taps and a "no" indicated by silence.[7] This apparent communication with "the unseen" became a broad public spectacle, and many witnesses thought it undeniable that the sisters had revealed evidence of the existence of a ghost. Later, it became a popular belief that the ghostly responses were those of a peddler who had been murdered in the home.

Following the publicity of the Fox sisters' discovery, spiritualism in the United States was rekindled, and this upward trend continues today. A 1990 Gallup poll reported that 29 percent of Americans polled believe in ghosts. The same poll was again taken in 2001 where it was found that the belief in ghosts had risen to 42 percent.[8] In 2015, a PEW poll reported that 18 percent of the Americans polled stated they had actually witnessed a ghost.[9] This progressive increase is likely due, in part, to the popularity of television shows highlighting ghost phenomenon and the subsequent worldwide upsurge in ghost-hunting groups whose purposes are primarily to gather evidence of the existence of ghosts.

The advancement in technology also has played a role; digital photography now allows people to capture phenomena that have never before been documented, and state-of-the-art recording devices are able to capture electronic voice phenomena (EVPs) or voice recordings originating from unseen sources.

Though historically in the United States the belief in ghosts has waxed and waned, the legend of ghosts has persisted throughout the world and throughout time. Perhaps this is because we have never stopped experiencing them. Still, little is known about ghosts. What is the nature of ghosts? How do they come to be? Where do they belong? And who are they, what are they, and why are they here? Addressing these questions and more is the purpose of this book.

2

My Encounters with Ghosts

"When asked if I believe in ghosts, my answer is always the same; no, I have seen too many of them."[10]

—Samuel Johnson (1709–1784)

Mine is not a belief in ghosts but rather an acknowledgment of their existence. My acceptance of ghosts as a reality was long in coming and a journey that began at a young age. At age five, my family moved into a haunted house in a Chicago suburb. In many ways, ours was a typical home, a Victorian-era boarding house built in 1886. This was a two-story home with four bedrooms, a basement, an attic, and a small yard. Its only peculiarity was that it came with an occupant ghost. Unbeknownst to my family at the time, the home had been put up for rent following the death of the previous tenant. It wasn't until decades later that I learned the tenant had actually died in the home. I came to know her as Elizabeth.

As soon as we moved into the house, Elizabeth starting making contact with me. At night I would feel her stroke my hair. She would whisper in my ear and would knock things off my walls and shelves, particularly at night. Elizabeth would also scare my cat. I remember watching my cat appear to be watching someone or something walk by, and then she would dash off in the opposite direction. I remember the basement feeling incredibly creepy, so much so that in the twelve years I lived in the home, I do not recall once when I did not run up the basement stairs, heart pounding, slamming the door behind me with a great sense of relief when I did. As a rule, I tried to avoid the basement. I also remember, when I was about thirteen years old, being in my kitchen and having a distinct feeling of being watched. The sense of another presence there was so palpable that I made a mental note to myself that I remember this date. I told myself that it was a fact that there could be someone in the room who was unseen. Although I could not reconcile how or why this could be true, I knew it was. It became a truth to me on that day. Not long after that, this "fact" became more clear after Elizabeth showed herself to me.

I was fourteen and it was a warm summer afternoon. I was sitting in my bedroom listening to music when I looked up to see a woman standing about three feet in front of me—a transparent woman, no less. She appeared to be in her sixties. She was short, had curly grey hair, and was wearing a floral housedress. She was well defined, not wispy or vague. I did not see her through the corner of my eye, nor did she come and go in a flash. And our eyes locked. I felt as if I could not look away. We stared at each other for what seemed to be several minutes, although it's more likely to have been seconds. Then she did something that would ultimately change my life; she smiled at me. She gave a sideways, half-cocked, Mona Lisa-type grin. In that moment, I realized that I was witnessing something completely unknown to me. I understood that, whatever it was that I was observing, it was living, feeling, animated, and autonomous. In other words, it was something separate from me and not my imagination. That's when our eyes disengaged, and I left the room. I recognized that this event defied explanation and at the same time was undeniable. Though this experience felt overwhelming, I responded by walking away and telling no one of it. But I never forgot it.

When I was growing up in the 1960s and '70s, ghosts were not a subject openly discussed as a reality or, perhaps, an explanation for odd occurrences in a home. The subject of ghosts was relegated to the telling of tales while sitting around a campfire for the purpose of scaring one another prior to heading to bed.

At this time, it seemed that only the misguided and perhaps the richly imaginative believed in ghosts. Because I had not been exposed to anyone who acknowledged ghosts as possibly real, I never identified any of the activity in my home as ghostly. Instead, I would create my own explanations for these events; all of which, looking back, were blatantly irrational. I called this process of inventing explanations my "exercise in mental gymnastics." Because I could not come up with rational explanations for the paranormal activity in my house, I was forced to twist and contort my sense of logic in order to create explanations for what was going on that would satisfy me enough that I could find peace and feel at ease in my home. After that, my only challenge was to never question my explanations. Of course, this became more difficult as my reasoning abilities matured with age and as the activity in the home increased.

> "Ghosts are an apparition of a dead person which is believed to appear or become manifest in the living, typically as a nebulous image. Spirits are the nonphysical part of a person which is the seat of emotions and character; the soul."
>
> —James Murray (1837–1915), editor, *Oxford English Dictionary*

The year after Elizabeth appeared to me, I had my second encounter with a ghost when my sister and I spent a long-weekend vacation on a Native American burial ground. Early one morning, my sister and I awoke to find a young, Native American woman, in full Native American garb, leaning over me as I slept. She had long brown hair and was wearing a traditional Native American leather dress. She appeared to be about twenty years old. As she leaned over me, she appeared to be looking through me. I looked back and was silent again, not understanding what it was I was witnessing. My sister, being disoriented by the experience, asked her if she needed something. She did not respond and, in fact, remained completely still. After a few minutes, we both went back to sleep. We never mentioned this to anyone.

Two years later, I moved from my childhood home to the Pacific Northwest. About six weeks after my arrival to the area, I visited Mt. St. Helens in Washington state (prior to its 1980 eruption). There I went to Spirit Lake, a beautiful lake situated at the base of the mountain, and I witnessed two more spirits.

I was on a college retreat with several students and professors. Seven of us, including a professor, witnessed this first spirit together. This spirit appeared as a very white light with distinct parameters. It was the size and shape of a ten-year-old child and moved in a childlike manner. We watched as it walked in circles and appeared to skip joyfully. At one point it looked as if it was climbing in an upward motion only to start to slide downward as if slipping. This was all happening just above the lake's surface. We watched as it moved atop the lake for about fifteen minutes, walking in circles, skipping, and wandering. Suddenly, it appeared to freeze. It then rose toward the sky about twenty feet and vanished. We were all so moved by the experience that we began to hug one another but we said very little. Some were moved to tears. This too was beyond my understanding but at least here I had several other witnesses.

Later the same evening, I saw a second spirit. As I was sitting in a cabin, peering through a large picture window overlooking Spirit Lake with Mt. St. Helens in the background, I noticed a young Native American woman, appearing to be about twenty years old, among the trees. She was reminiscent of the Native American woman I saw months prior on the Indian burial ground. She was dancing. I watched as she hopped and skipped in circles with her head thrown back, looking toward the sky with arms open. I watched as she would fall to her knees and bow, then get back up, arch her back, and twirl in circles as she pointed to the sky. I watched her for about twenty minutes before I made a decision I would come to regret. I left the room to go to bed. To this day, I wish I hadn't. I wish I had stayed to see what else could have manifested, but that was a lot to take in for one day, and, after all, I was only seventeen.

This time, I spoke of my paranormal experience. After encountering this fourth spirit, I could no longer remain quiet and dismiss my experiences as being "unexplainable." Now I could explain them. What I had been experiencing since childhood was contact with ghosts and other spirits. It all made perfect sense. A ghost had been whispering in my ear as a child, stroking my hair, frightening the cat, giving me the sense of being watched, and causing the creepy feelings in my home. It was a ghost that was responsible for the items falling from my walls and shelves. It was a ghost I saw standing in my room. These were all evidence of ghosts being real and any mental gymnastics to explain these experiences away had been nothing more than a practice of lying to myself to create peace of mind. I was so energized by this epiphany that I ran to my room and started journaling every event that could now be explained as ghostly and as connecting with the dead.

For decades I continued to write about my paranormal experiences, both as I recalled them and as I continue to experience them. Early on in this practice, I realized that although this newfound understanding helped me make sense of my childhood experiences, I still had more questions than answers. I wanted to understand ghosts. I wanted to know their habits and emotions, their awareness and abilities, their thoughts and desires. In contemplating how to study ghosts I realized I first needed to study death—death as a transition.

3

Who They Are

"In order to be a ghost a choice must be made."[11]

—Diana Palm, *Setting Spirits Free*

Death is a natural, normal, and healthy process of transition from the physical world into a new world of opportunity. Ghosts are a product of those who got stuck along the way. People are often surprised to learn that when we die we remain exactly as we were before we died in personality, disposition, temperament, moods, values, dreams and goals, beliefs and understandings, tastes, preferences, talents, memories, sense of humor, and so on. This is because when we die *we* do not change; our circumstances do. To illustrate this, I like to compare those who go from life into death to a scuba diver who goes from land into water. Once a scuba diver jumps into the water, they have entered a new world where fundamental things are different. For example, their interplay with gravity dramatically changes. In water we can go up, down, back and forth, and can do somersaults and cartwheels, and cannot fall. Motion is different underwater, considerably slowed down; virtually nothing can be done quickly underwater. Likewise, the ability to communicate is essentially nonexistent and our senses function differently. We can no longer see or hear without distortion, and can't smell or taste at all. Whereas all these factors change upon entering the water, we don't change a bit, not in personality, disposition, temperament, mood, values, dreams and goals, beliefs and understanding, sense of humor, and so on. This is because, when we enter the water we don't change but our circumstances do. And the reason for this is simple; it is because we are spirit now, and so as spirit we begin our transition.

To understand death as a transition, it helps to take a look at what the near-death experience (NDE) has taught us. Researchers Kenneth Ring, PhD, and Raymond A. Moody, MD, PhD, raised awareness and increased the conversation about NDEs after publishing their research on the subject in the 1970s and '80s.[12] This research included interviews with subjects who claimed to have had extraordinary experiences during their brief clinical "deaths." Most people today know of NDEers who describe experiences of having been in contact with deceased loved ones or of seeing a light, for example. Most people, however, are not aware that the death transition is a five-stage process. Once the heart stops beating, breathing ceases, and there are no more electrical impulses to the brain, we begin our journey into the first stage of the transition.

"There is no so-called death but rather a transition from the visible into invisible worlds."[13]

— Carl Wickland,
Thirty Years Among the Dead

Stages of the Death Transition[14]

1. Feeling a Sense of Peace and Well-Being
Following the death of the body, we enter the first stage of transition, which is marked by a sense of well-being and a lack of pain. NDEers commonly describe feeling calm, peaceful, carefree, and warm. They note that the sense of peace and well-being increases as they move further into the transition.

2. Feeling Separate from the Body
In the second stage of transition our awareness shifts. Our focal point of awareness is no longer associated with the body but rather becomes independent of it, having moved from being centered in the face and

head region to now being situated somewhere else in the immediate environment. Many NDEers report feeling as if they lifted out of their body and then finding themselves hovering above it. Some report watching their resuscitation and have given accurate descriptions of events that transpired during their (momentary) deaths. During this stage, we become no longer "of the physical world" yet remain within it.

3. Encountering a Tunnel
While in the third stage, a tunnel presents itself. NDEers consistently describe a large, round-shaped tunnel with a bright light at its end. During this stage, and throughout the five stages, there is what has been described as a magnetic-type pull that gently guides us through the tunnel and beyond. This magnetic pull reportedly does not force or interfere with free will.

4. Encountering a Light
At the end of the tunnel is a light. This light has been described as yellow, golden, and white in color. It has been deemed by those who encounter it as much more than a light and characterized as a living being such as God, Buddha, Jesus, Love, Truth, and Oneness, to name a few. Those who have experienced this fourth stage report a compelling desire to move into the light. In my own NDE research,[15] one of the features unanimously reported among our participants was that the light was the destination.

5. The Inner Setting

The fifth and final stage is called the "inner setting." Here, one has entered "into the light." NDEers speak of seeing their deceased loved ones and others familiar to them. This fifth stage marks the end of the transition and previous physical life and the beginning of a new life in a new field of opportunity, in a place that has its own laws of physics.

4

Becoming a Ghost

"Ghosts are a condition of the spirit that can occur at death as a result of the mental and emotional state of the recently deceased."[16]

—DIANA PALM, *SETTING SPIRITS FREE*

In 2019, prior to the COVID-19 pandemic, 55 million people had died worldwide. That translates into approximately 150,000 having died each day, worldwide that year.[17] Given this statistic, it is fair to say that ghosts represent a small fraction of that figure. One reason ghosts are rare is because the death transition can be a passive experience. It is often described as profoundly easy. Most NDEers describe it as feeling very natural and as a joyful event. Even so, some people who die get stalled in the transition and fail to move through the five stages. They get caught in the second stage, causing them to remain earthbound, which brings me to the story of one of my NDE study participants. Her name was Carol.

Carol was an NDEer whom I had the pleasure of interviewing. Carol was a woman who had an NDE at age fifty, following a heart attack. She described the events following her heart attack, stating she recalled having severe chest pain and calling 911. She remembered the paramedics coming to her home, quickly assessing her, and placing her on a gurney. She said as they were walking her out to the waiting ambulance, she suddenly began feeling peaceful and calm and was no longer experiencing pain (First Stage: Feelings of Peace and Well Being). She said the next thing she knew, she had the sense she was walking alongside the paramedics. She described viewing her body lying on the gurney and watching her resuscitation (Second Stage: Sense of Being Separate From the Body). I asked Carol what she was thinking and feeling when she noticed she was able to view her body, and Carol said she was annoyed. She told me she was yelling at the paramedics, "I'm here! I'm here! I am right here!" and said she thought they were ignoring her.

Fortunately for Carol, she was resuscitated and lived to tell her story, but what if she hadn't been? What if the resuscitation had failed and Carol remained focused on her physical surroundings to the point that, through her own free will, she essentially neglected to move into the third, fourth, and fifth stages of the death transition? Then Carol would have been a ghost. And what if Carol continued to seek the attention of those around her and realized that her voice was not getting a response? What if she then decided to experiment with the physical world to see if she could create an effect that would get her the attention she sought? Well, then Carol would have been a ghost who haunted.

Though the vast majority of those who die complete their transition, a small percentage do not. Those who get stalled in the process we call ghosts. The failure to transition can be reduced to one common factor: the deceased being unprepared to die. It is important to note that many people who die unprepared do not become ghosts, however, of those who do, one thing they have in common is the lack of preparation for their deaths.

Near-death-experiencers have broadly described the death transition as a natural, normal, peaceful, and joyful event with these states only intensifying as they move forward through the stages. But, as discussed, some of the recently deceased choose to remain in the familiar setting of the physical world and become ghosts. Ghosts tend to result from deaths that were sudden and unexpected, such as those by murder, accident, or short-term illness. Ghosts occur less frequently from deaths by old age or long-term illness. (Incidents of ghosts by means of suicide are unknown.) It is our emotional and mental state at the time of our deaths that cause the disruption of a smooth transition whereby the recently deceased ultimately choose not to move forward and resist the transition experience.

The basis for this resistance is as individual as the individual ghost, but the reason generally falls into one of three categories: they are fearful of moving forward in the transition, they are confused by what they are experiencing, they hold a passionate desire to complete something on earth, or any combination of the three.

Some may be fearful simply because what they are experiencing is unfamiliar to them. They also may be fearful because they believe they haven't lived up to certain expectations, such as through their religious training, and are fearful of potential consequences. Some are confused because they have no understanding of what is happening to them. I have found some in this category to be under the impression they are in a coma, a dream state, or in a drug-induced state, for example. Those who hold no concept of life after death may be among the confused. There are also those who remain earthbound due to their passion to complete something on earth. This could be a mother who died in childbirth wanting to remain with her baby, or an executive who launched a long-awaited business they desire to oversee, or any other passion a person may hold. No matter what the motivation, it is the application of free will that allows it to happen. In addition, lack of information, or misinformation about death can cause fear, confusion, and the belief that by remaining earthbound after death one can satisfy earthly passions. Following are some examples of the ghosts with whom I have worked who represent the three reasons ghosts remain earthbound.

5

Alfred—A Ghost of Passion

I had been going to a movie theater in my hometown for nearly a decade when one evening I felt I was in the presence of a ghost. As I was going to my seat, I became acutely aware of a tall, thin, middle-aged man wearing a cape and top hat standing next to me in the aisle. Though I had been involved in the "ghost community" in the area, I had not been made aware of a ghostly presence at the theater. A few days later, I returned and asked the theater staff if any of them had ever experienced paranormal activity. Several stated they were fully aware that the theater had an occupant ghost and reported seeing objects move, hearing voices, feeling breath on their necks, and having a sense of being watched. They reported that the presence was most active at closing and several of the employees refused to work the night shift; some were so frightened by it they quit. I came to know the occupant ghost as Alfred.

I sensed Alfred was a kind and gentle soul and asked the theater manager if I could invite ghost hunting groups to the theater for investigation. I was given permission and my first group visited a few weeks later. Some of the theater employees agreed to participate in the investigation, and we gathered in the theater basement. During our attempt to communicate with Alfred, which we audio recorded, we asked him questions in hopes of capturing electronic voice phenomena (EVPs) or audio recordings from a frequency not otherwise heard by humans. As it turned out, we received several EVPs indicating we were, in fact, communicating with an unseen source.

From my assessment of Alfred, I determined he died at about age forty in approximately 1939 and that he was passionate about theater, vaudeville theater in particular. Alfred believed he was murdered because he was homosexual; I believe he died of an accidental opiate overdose. This discrepancy was not important, however. What mattered was that Alfred became a ghost because he so loved the performing arts that he wanted to remain in the theater, where he had died.

Of particular interest to me was what Alfred said when we asked him if there was anything we could do for him. A clear reply could be heard: "Yes." When we asked him to be more specific, he said, "Home." I concluded that Alfred wanted help getting out of his current condition and wanted to find his "home" after wandering as a ghost for some sixty years. Feeling compelled to help Alfred, I requested permission from the theater staff to do a clearing for him to assist him into the inner setting.

To my amazement, the staff rejected my proposal. They said they had become more comfortable with Alfred's presence following our investigation and were no longer "creeped out" by him. They said they viewed him as a kind soul who was looking out for them. This put me in a quandary. Though this characterization of Alfred may have been true, I believed Alfred had reached out for help and I wanted to honor his desire. Feeling that I couldn't do so without the staff's permission, I pled my case again. This then prompted one of the staff members, who had participated in our ghost investigation, to do something brilliant. With an audio recorder in hand, she asked Alfred what he thought about my returning to the theater and working with him. He clearly responded, "Good." After the theater staff heard this EVP, they allowed me to perform a clearing. Nine years later, the staff reported that they had not sensed a ghost in the theater since the clearing.

6

Steve—A Fear-Based Ghost

Fear can cause a paralysis in energetic flow at the time of death, which can cause us to remain in this world though belonging to the next. Those who resist the death transition because of fear may do so out of fear of atonement, judgment, or simply fear of the unknown. One of my favorite ghosts to work with was a fear-based ghost named Steve.

I met Steve through a young woman we'll call Beth, who lived in a neighboring town. One night Beth called me in distress. As it turned out, Beth was living in an apartment that was well known to be haunted. She said she had been living in her home with a ghost peacefully for about a year when he suddenly began threatening her. She said she heard him swear at her and call her names, and he would angrily tell her guests to get out of the house. Beth said he had become very noisy, slamming doors and cupboards and actively haunting her home. She was so frightened by this that she had been staying elsewhere for several weeks. I agreed to assist her and, at her instance, we met that very night outside her home.

When I entered Beth's home, I immediately felt the ghost's presence. My assessment of Steve was that he had committed suicide in the bedroom area. I suspected it happened about fifteen years prior. Beth was able to verify his name and means of death. I sensed that Steve recognized he had died and stayed behind out of fear of moving forward. I felt that Steve believed his ex-wife was deceased and, for reasons of his own, he harbored guilt related to her death. I believed Steve was a ghost concerned about moving through the transition because he did not feel secure in his fate. I did not concern myself with how his wife had died, whether it was through a violent act at Steve's hands or an accident for which he felt responsible, for example, because I felt it didn't matter. I sensed his wife was waiting for him. My message to Steve was that he needn't be afraid because his wife was waiting for him and he was free to go to her.

After I felt Steve depart and completed my clearing, I called Beth and invited her to return home. I did not tell her anything about my time with Steve, including that he was earthbound out of fear and guilt over the death of his wife or that I encouraged him to go to her. I told Beth only that he was no longer present. Beth, who was not yet aware she had psychic mediumship skills herself, immediately felt an energetic shift in her home. She said it felt "lighter" in her home, she could sense he was gone, and she now felt she could live peacefully in her home again.

As sometimes happens, when talking with Beth that night, I felt compelled to give her a message. I told her that she would have a dream about Steve that would hold an important message and I wanted her to pay attention to it. I was unsure why this message was important but gained clarification the following day when Beth called me. She said Steve did come to her in a dream and said, "I am sorry I scared you. I didn't want to hurt you. I have to go now; she's waiting for me." The only way Beth could have known there was a woman waiting for him was if Steve himself had told her. The fact that Steve came to her in such a manner demonstrated that a ghost is capable of moving from a physical location (a home) into a dream setting, and then into the beyond. Thus illustrating the flexibility and expanded potential of a freed spirit. I found this ghost experience exceptional for another reason. As it turned out, Steve's apology to Beth helped her to acknowledge her mediumship skills and to understand ghosts on a different level.

About a year after the clearing, I received a thank-you note from Beth who said she continued to be comfortable living in her home. She also shared that, since her dream of Steve, she had continued to be sensitive to ghosts and had grown to understand that ghosts have distinct personalities as they did prior to death and that they perhaps do not need to be feared. Beth wrote that she has since embraced her psychic mediumship talents and will at times assist in clearing them.

7

Ben—A Ghost in Confusion

*Some ghosts feel they have popped out of
the body and are in a strange circumstance
where they are ignored.*[18]

—GARY HILL LEON, *PEOPLE THAT DON'T
KNOW THEY ARE DEAD*

A certain percentage of people find they are confused at the point of death. They may have no frame of reference for death being a transition and cannot fathom what is happening. They may feel completely disorientated by the experience. Often those who are confused come to believe they must be in a dream state, under the influence of drugs, or in a coma, for example. This was the case with a ghost I call Ben.

Ben was in his early forties when he died in a work-related accident due to some sort of explosion. This, of course, was an unexpected and jarring event for him. He was a ghost who believed he was in some sort of a coma as he wandered around the home of a young woman, Melissa, to whom he became attached.

Ben's dream in life had been to have a wife and family, and he continued to try to attain this through Melissa. Melissa told me she could often feel his presence and sometimes could hear him breathing. She said she would find things rearranged in her home and that he would open and close doors. On one occasion, Melissa believed he had appeared at night as a cloud-like mist hovering over her bed.

I believe that Ben was haunting inadvertently as he went about his business, trying to find fulfillment as best he could through making contact with Melissa. My work with Ben was to address his confusion and educate him about his circumstances. I essentially oriented him to the fact that he was not dreaming, that this was not a drug-induced state nor a coma, and that, in fact, he had died. I then introduced him to the idea that there was a path available to a new environment where he could find the fulfillment he desired. Ben was a ghost who appeared to be eager to understand the transition available to him. Once he did, he left immediately. When I contacted Melissa months after the clearing, she said she was living peacefully and no longer felt his presence.

Another example of ghosts in confusion was two young girls who appeared to me at my bedside one morning. I had never had ghosts approach me in this manner. These two sisters, whom I call Liz and Nancy, were about eleven and thirteen years old. One died in an accident, and the other, from illness. They asked me if I "was the doctor." I was startled by their presence and their inquiry confounded me until I took the time to pay attention to what they were asking. They were looking for a doctor. I believed they had some degree of awareness that I could help, though not a doctor. Having died from illness and from an accident, they thought what they needed was a doctor, when what they really needed was clarification about their circumstances. Once this was clear to me, I was able to assist them by making them aware that they had died, educating them about their current situation, and encouraging them to move into the inner setting.

8

What Ghosts Are

In simplest terms, during our transition, the spirit can differentiate itself into parts; one of which can exist as a ghost part. If people are made up of consciousness with flesh and bones, then ghosts are made up of consciousness and ectoplasm.

Ectoplasm is the molecular substance that makes up the ghost "body." It is the transparent, gray-white, filmy type substance captured in ghost photos and what is sometimes seen with the naked eye. Ectoplasm can change shape and can present as a mist or cloud or as a recognizable form such as that of a person.

The ghost form (or body) is organized based on what the ghost identifies with at any particular moment. For example, if a ghost identifies as having been in a tragic accident (such as one that caused their death), their ectoplasm will organize in a manner that represents this event. At this time, they may appear with injuries and torn clothes, or the like. Or, if a ghost identifies as being a bride, she may appear in a wedding gown and veil. If one identifies with having been a solider, they may present in a military uniform and so on. So, whatever they are holding in their consciousness as their self-identity at a given time is what their ectoplasm will reflect. For ghosts, form literally follows thought. If they are not identifying with any particular presentation, the ectoplasm may present as disorganized and more like a cloud or fog.

Ghosts do not seek food or shelter or rest to obtain the energy they need to subsist. Rather, they are entirely reliant on the physical environment for energy and for their ability to be animated. They draw their energy from three sources: people, animals, and electronic currents. This energy then allows them the ability to appear to us, touch us, move objects, and disrupt electrical currents related to objects such as computers, microwaves, and televisions, for example. In my research, I have learned that ghosts maintain the ability to see and hear, though I have not seen evidence of their ability to smell or taste. They can certainly touch us, but whether or not they have tactile sensations when doing so is unclear. Ghosts' senses function differently than they did when embodied. Again, this shift can be compared to a scuba diver who sees and hears with less clarity once underwater. Based on my communications with the other side, I have concluded that ghosts also hear and see the physical world with less clarity and see people primarily as energy and less as a physical form. For this reason, it is difficult for them to intrude on our privacy as they primarily see the physical world obscured by the energy fields that surround it.

Because people are one of the sources from which they draw energy, they can deplete us, causing us to feel drained from the ghost's presence. For this reason, it is not healthy to be in the presence of ghosts, as they can strip us of our vitality and it is our vitality that maintains health and prevents illness. This is why people, not just ghosts, are better off once a ghost moves out of any shared proximity and into their natural home of the inner setting.

Further, ectoplasm is a physical substance and will eventually deteriorate. This is a problem for ghosts because it means they will eventually lose the ability to take form. The total degradation of ectoplasm is said to take approximately a century. Though awareness can withstand without form, without ectoplasm ghosts can have a difficult time communicating with the physical world. Once a ghost enters the inner setting, the physical substance of ectoplasm transforms, as it is no longer a necessary particulate of the spirit anatomy.

Some ghosts become attuned to psychics, with whom they have the best chance of communicating. They can do this by observing that people (as well as animals) are responding to their presence. For example, Elizabeth, the ghost in my childhood home, would have been able to see that when she whispered in my ear I would turn my head toward her and when she stroked my hair I would respond by rubbing my head. They are also capable of learning who holds psychic abilities by observing the energetic fields that surround us (our auras) and deciphering what the energetic patterns indicate, such as mediumship skills. Psychic mediums possess a particular intensity of light within the aura that acts as a beacon to ghosts. Of course, whether the psychic acknowledges the ghost or their psychic abilities is up to them, but knowledgeable ghosts are likely to seek them out for information and to send messages to the living.

9

Ghosts Versus Spirits

"When a ghost is crossed over into the light, it raises its vibration and becomes a "spirit."[19]

—Diana Palm, *Setting Spirits Free*

Ghosts and spirits are different entities. Ghosts are a fragment of the spirit that is stuck in an earthbound state. Spirits are integrated into the realm of their natural home and are more free to roam.

People often use the terms *spirit* and *ghost* interchangeably. This is no more accurate comparison than using the terms "fruit" and "apples" interchangeably. Apples are fruit but not all fruit are apples. Similarly, ghosts are spirits but not all spirits are ghosts.

Ghosts are the emotional aspect of the human spirit that remains behind. For this reason, ghosts tend to be emotionally charged. If in life, for example, the deceased was a demure, shy individual, then as a ghost they will tend to be less so. Similarly, if the deceased had an angry, aggressive personality in life, then as a ghost they will tend to be even more angry and more aggressive. Ghosts also tend to have foggy cognition, which perhaps can be compared to when we first wake up in the morning and are somewhat disoriented. Ghosts are ethereal and timeless; for them, everything is happening now and they have no concept of the past or future. Ghosts are known to be transparent, slow-moving, and "creepy." Their state of existence tends to be dreary, confused, and monotonous.[20] They do not move between worlds and may lack the awareness of a spirit world into which they can enter. In this way, they are stuck in their circumstances and are reliant on whatever the physical environment presents for the acquisition of information, including that of their current circumstances. Unfortunately for them, the access to such information can be extremely limited.

Non-ghost spirits, on the contrary, are not highly emotional by nature and tend to have sharp cognition. They are made of light and are not always transparent. They are integrated into their natural environments, can travel freely between worlds, and move in real-time. Also unlike ghosts, they do not drain our energy or give off a creepy vibe and they do not haunt. Instead, people generally tend to feel neutral or inspired when in the presence of non-ghost spirits.

What they have in common includes being aware and having the ability to reason. Neither have pain sensors and, therefore, experience no pain. Both can be seen with the naked eye or through psychic abilities, and both can communicate with us in dreams, through telepathy, and by speaking, touching, and appearing to us.

10

Why We Fear Ghosts

"The oldest and strongest emotion of mankind is fear, and the oldest and strongest kind of fear is fear of the unknown."[21]

—H. P. LOVECRAFT

Though the concept of ghosts is ancient, they continue to be shrouded in mystery and many myths surround them. Until they are better understood, humankind is likely to continue to fear them. I have come to appreciate this fear because being in the presence of ghosts is not healthy for us, due to their proclivity for depleting our energy, therefore we are better off outside their presence. However, in my exploration of ghosts, I have found that they lack the energy and talent needed to cause people significant harm. I have not known ghosts to break bones, cause bruising, knock a person down, choke them, or in any way cause significant injury. For a ghost to accomplish such a feat is virtually impossible because it would take the confluence of three factors: the desire to harm, the building of skills needed to inflict harm, and access to the concentration of energy needed to create enough force to cause an injury.

Though there are ghosts who wish us harm (I have met a few), they would need to maintain that desire for decades while practicing the skills needed to execute significant harm. For a ghost to gather the knowledge and strength needed to cross from the ghost world into the physical world can be compared to us crossing into "another world" by defying gravity and accomplishing levitation. Some would say this can be done, but most would say it is, at best, an exceptionally rare occurrence. Furthermore, unlike us, ghosts need to draw and harness a great deal of energy from their environment to execute anything that could cause us significant harm. This level of energy is not something readily available to them. Ghosts are generally ineffective at impacting the physical world. This may come as a particularly sad realization for ghosts of passion who remain earthbound for the purposes of completing unfinished business. Ghosts only have one talent for impacting the physical world: they scare us, whether they intend to or not. And in this area, they are experts.

I believe that this fear is driven by three factors. One is the fear of the unknown. We know little about them, including their capabilities and intentions, so being in close proximity to a ghost can be unnerving, to say the least. The second is the depiction of ghosts in books, movies, and other productions as mysterious, dangerous, volatile, and something to avoid. They are often portrayed as being capable of committing heinous acts upon us. The third is something that I don't hear spoken of often and could be the undercurrent of our collective fear—which is that they run at a frequency that causes us to feel unsettled in their presence. A ghost's energy is measurable through what ghost adventurers call an EMF, or an Electric Magnetic Field detector. This device not only can indicate that a ghost is present but also determine the strength of their energetic field. I contend that ghosts run at a vibratory rate (or frequency) that naturally causes us angst. I compare this frequency with the minor keys in music. Music is in itself benign and cannot cause us harm but it is highly effective at evoking emotion, including fear. I theorize that ghosts, like music, run at a frequency comparable to minor keys in music, thus causing a creepy feeling. This is something that comes naturally to them. They will continue to run at this frequency so long as they remain in the ghost state. Once in the inner setting, their frequency increases, changing their vibration.

11

Why They Haunt

Ghosts have two means by which they haunt, inadvertently and with intention. Hauntings are defined as any occurrence whereby ghosts make their presence known. And this haunting is, whether intentional or not, generally met with fear. Ghosts often make their presence known accidentally when going about their business, unaware they are crossing into the physical dimension. Some may not understand how this happens, while others intentionally cross into the physical world and master the manipulation of objects to create effects in our environment at will. If ghosts remain in the presence of people long enough, they will eventually haunt.

Often they try to make contact with us to simply let us know they are there or in an effort to get us to provide a service for them, such as helping them to escape their current circumstance (that of being a ghost) or to deliver a message to a loved one. They also may make contact to scare us. This could be out of simple mischief or for a specific purpose, such as to drive us out of a home in an effort to reclaim it. Typically this strategy is effective.

In one such case, I worked with a ghost named Marcus who had learned to terrify a family in my neighborhood so profoundly that he drove them out of their home. The homeowner called me to ask for my assistance. She said Marcus would slam doors, knock things over, give off an intensely angry vibe that people could feel in their home, and had appeared as a disembodied head to people in the home. He terrified the family so much that they fled and did not live in, or rent out, the home for two years. His anger was palpable, and his energy was high enough to create a ruckus in the home. Marcus created the highest electromagnetic "disturbances" I had ever seen—causing my electromagnetic field indicator to go to its highest capacity, red.

The family asked me to clear the home, which I did. Through my work, I learned that Marcus had died in a gang-related shooting and was angry about his death and wanted justice. My work with Marcus included letting him know that this "worldly" concern for justice was now ours, not his burden, and he was free to rest. In the case of Marcus, the family had been so traumatized by his presence that they never returned to the home, instead choosing to sell it.

12

Why They Remain

"Instead of looking at the smudge on the window, look through the window."[22]

—GARY HILL LEON, *PEOPLE WHO DON'T KNOW THEY ARE DEAD*

Ghosts remain earthbound because they are stuck, having temporarily lost their ability to perceive the spiritual aspect of what they are experiencing, causing them to lose their way. This "stuckness" is a principle component of being a ghost. If not for being stuck, they would be capable of traveling between worlds and would no longer be a ghost but rather a free spirit. This stuckness is known to occur approximately three days after death if the deceased remains earthbound, having neglected to move past the second stage of the death transition. When the deceased is focused on the physical world to the exclusion of moving beyond it, they will eventually lose the ability to perceive their way forward. This includes being unable to enter the pathway into the inner setting (the third, fourth, and fifth stages). Additionally, they are unable to utilize the assistance that has come forward on their behalf from the spirit world. This is similar to reports from people who have been trapped in darkness for periods of time; they find that when they resurface they are unable to perceive their new surroundings because their eyes have become so attuned to the dark. In the same way, if the deceased in the second stage of the transition remains focused on the physical world long enough, their consciousness will remain attuned to that world and the spiritual side of their experience (including the final three stages) becomes imperceivable. Though outside their perception, they remain energetically tethered to these final stages and to the spirit world.

Not understanding their new reality is a particularly difficult problem for ghosts, so they often look to us, and to the physical world, to assist them. The key to moving forward in the transition relies on awakening their consciousness. If they can acknowledge there is a way out of their current circumstance, they will then have a renewed ability to perceive it. We often hear the phrase, "When I see it, I will believe it." For ghosts, it is more accurate to say, "When I believe it, I will see it." Once convinced there is something there to perceive, their "eyes" (or consciousness) will open, making it possible to enter the inner setting.

A comparable example of this can be seen in the story, *The Wizard of Oz*. Here the central character, Dorothy, embarks on a great adventure in an attempt to find her way home when, in fact, she had the power, through her ruby slippers, to go home all along. Dorothy had been unaware of this until Glinda the Good Witch "awakened her to it." Once Dorothy acknowledged she had the means to go home, she was able to successfully get there. The same goes for ghosts. In order for ghosts to perceive the final stages of their transition, they need to acknowledge that something is there to guide them through the transition and into the inner setting. Once they become aware of this possibility, they will be able to complete the final stages.

13

Completing the Transition

Ghosts do not thrive when earthbound. Here they are in a predicament because not only are they now a part of the spirit world yet living in the physical world, but they are also stuck here. They are like sea turtles who find themselves on land, unable to find a body of water. Such turtles can get by for a period of time, but they cannot thrive and grow and be all they are meant to be unless they are in their natural environment; the sea. Likewise, ghosts will only thrive once they are in the natural environment of the inner setting where transformation can bring them into their fullness as spirits. Ghosts need to move into the light of the inner setting for ectoplasm to transform into light, and for them to become integrated spirits continuing in their spiritual evolution. During this journey, consciousness expands and enables the integration of the freed spirit to emerge with expanded capabilities. From the inner setting, they have the ability to thrive. No longer in a dreary state of being, they can live in peace.

SELECTED RESOURCES

Alexander, Eben. *Proof of Heaven: A Neurosurgeon's Journey Into the Afterlife.* New York: Simon and Schuster, 2012.

Fiore, Edith. *The Unquiet Dead: A Psychologist Treats Spirit Possession.* New York: Ballantine Books, 1995.

Graham, Jed. "An Ancient Ghost Story by Pliny the Younger." History of Yesterday website. Last modified July 20, 2020. Accessed June 29, 2020. https://historyofyesterday.com/an-ancient-ghost-story-by-pliny-the-younger-cbe8011ecbca.

Greyson, Bruce. "Near-Death Studies, 1981–82: A Review." *Anabiosis—The Journal for Near-Death Studies* 2, no. 2 (1982): 150–58.

Hinkle, Irving. *The First Ghosts: Most Ancient of Legacies.* Reprint. London: Hodder and Stoughton, 2023.

Leon, Gary Hill. *People Who Don't Know They Are Dead: How They Attach Themselves to Unsuspecting Bystanders and What to Do About It.* Newburyport, MA: Weiser Books, 2005.

Lindley, James H., Bryan, Sethyn, and Conley, Bob. "Near-Death-Experience in a Pacific Northwest American Population: The Evergreen Study." *Anabiosis—The Journal for Near-Death Studies* 1, no. 2 (1981): 104–24.

Lovecraft, H. P. *Supernatural Horror in Literature.* Bristol: Read and Co. Books, 2020, 1.

Ring, Kenneth. *Life at Death: A Scientific Investigation of the Near-Death Experience.* New York: Coward-McCann, 1980.

Roser, Max. "Causes of Death Globally: What Do People Die From?" Our World in Data website, last updated December 8, 2021, accessed December 23, 2021, https://ourworldindata.org/causes-of-death-treemap.

Tompkins, Ptolemy. *The Modern Book of the Dead: A Revolutionary Perspective on Death, the Soul, and What Really Happens in the Life to Come.* New York: Atria Publishing, 2013).

Trotman, Wayne Gerard. *Veterans of the Psychic Wars.* Pittsburgh, PA: Red Moon Productions, 2015.

Weisberg, Barbara. *Talking to the Dead: Kate and Maggie Fox and the Rise of Spiritualism.* New York: HarperOne, 2009).

Wickland, Carl. *Thirty Years Among the Dead.* Surrey: White Crow Books, 2011.

BIBLIOGRAPHY

Alexander, Eben. *Proof of Heaven: A Neurosurgeon's Journey Into the Afterlife.* New York: Simon and Schuster, 2012.

Irving Hinkle, Irving. *The First Ghosts: Most Ancient of Legacies.* London: Hodder and Stoughton, 2023.

Kachuba, John. *The Missing Peace in Your Life.* Crestone, CO: Myrdinn Publications, 2004.

Lipka, Michael "18% of Americans say they've seen a ghost" Pew Research Center, October 30, 2015. https://www.pewresearch.org/short-reads/2015/10/30/18-of-americans-say-theyve-seen-a-ghost/

Leon, Gary Hill. *People Who Don't Know They Are Dead: How They Attach Themselves to Unsuspecting Bystanders and What to Do About It.* Newburyport, MA: Weiser Books, 2005.

Newport, Frank and Maria Strausberg. *Gallup News Service.* "Americans' Belief in Psychic and Paranormal Phenomena Is up Over Last Decade," June 2010. https://news.gallup.com/poll/4483/americans-belief-psychic-paranormal-phenomena-over-last-decade.aspx.

Palm, Diana. *Setting Spirits Free: Clear Negative Energy and Help Ghosts Cross Over.* Woodbury, MN: Lewelynn Publications, 2013.

Tompkins, Ptolemy. *Modern Book of the Dead*. New York: Atria Books, 2013.

Wickland, Carl. *Thirty Years Among the Dead*. Surrey: White Crow Books, 2011.

NOTES

1. John Kachuba, *The Missing Peace in Your Life* (Crestone, CO: Myrdinn Publications, 2004).
2. Eben Alexander, MD, *Proof of Heaven* (New York: Simon and Schuster, 2012): 1.
3. Irving Hinkle, *The First Ghosts: Most Ancient of Legacies*, Reprint (London: Hodder and Stoughton, 2023): 1.
4. Jed Graham, "An Ancient Ghost Story by Pliny the Younger," History of Yesterday website, last modified July 20, 2020, accessed June 29, 2020, https://historyofyesterday.com/an-ancient-ghost-story-by-pliny-the-younger-cbe8011ecbca.
5. Ptolemy Tompkins, *The Modern Book of the Dead: A Revolutionary Perspective on Death, the Soul, and What Really Happens in the Life to Come* (New York: Atria Publishing, 2013): 150.
6. Ptolemy Tompkins, *Modern Book of the Dead* (New York: Atria Books, 2013): 150.
7. Barbara Weisberg, *Talking to the Dead: Kate and Maggie Fox and the Rise of Spiritualism* (New York: HarperOne, 2009): 20.
8. Frank Newport and Maria Strausberg, "Americans' Belief in Psychic and Paranormal Phenomena Is up Over Last Decade," *Gallup News Service* (June

2010). https://news.gallup.com/poll/4483/americans-belief-psychic-paranormal-phenomena-over-last-decade.aspx.
9 Michael Lipka, "18% of Americans say they've seen a ghost" Pew Research Center, (October 30, 2015). https://www.pewresearch.org/short-reads/2015/10/30/18-of-americans-say-theyve-seen-a-ghost/.
10 Carl Wickland, *Thirty Years Among the Dead* (Surrey: White Crow Books, 2011): 148.
11 Diana Palm, *Setting Spirits Free: Clear Negative Energy and Help Ghosts Cross Over* (Woodbury, MN: Lewelynn Publications, 2013): 33.
12 Kenneth Ring, *Life at Death: A Scientific Investigation of the Near-Death Experience* (New York: Coward-McCann, 1980).
13 Carl Wickland, *Thirty Years Among the Dead* (Surrey: White Crow Books, 2011), 29.
14 James H. Lindley, Sethyn Bryan, and Bob Conley, "Near-Death Experience in a Pacific Northwest American Population: The Evergreen Study," *Anabiosis—The Journal for Near-Death Studies* 1, no. 2 (1981): 104–24.
15 Ibid.
16 Diana Palm, *Setting Spirits Free: Clear Negative Energy and Help Ghosts Cross Over* (Woodbury, MN: Lewelynn Publications, 2013): 35.
17 Max Roser, "Causes of Death Globally: What Do People Die From?" Our World in Data website, last updated December 8, 2021, accessed

December 23, 2021, https://ourworldindata.org/causes-of-death-treemap.

18 Gary Hill Leon, *People Who Don't Know They Are Dead: How They Attach Themselves to Unsuspecting Bystanders and What to Do About It* (Newburyport, MA: Weiser Books, 2005): 27.

19 Diana Palm, *Setting Spirits Free: Clear Negative Energy and Help Ghosts Cross Over* (Woodbury, MN: Lewelynn Publications, 2013): 36.

20 Carl Wickland, *Thirty Years Among the Dead* (Surrey: White Crow Books, 2011): 69.

21 H. P. Lovecraft, *Supernatural Horror in Literature* (Bristol: Read and Co. Books, 2020): 1.

22 Gary Hill Leon, *People Who Don't Know They Are Dead: How They Attach Themselves to Unsuspecting Bystanders and What to Do About It* (Newburyport, MA: Weiser Books, 2005): 25.

23 Bruce Greyson, "Near-Death Studies, 1981–82: A Review," *Anabiosis—The Journal for Near-Death Studies* 2, no. 2 (1982): 150–58.

24 Eben Alexander, MD, *Proof of Heaven* (New York: Simon and Schuster, 2012): 1.

25 Irving Hinkle, *The First Ghosts: Most Ancient of Legacies*, Reprint (London: Hodder and Stoughton, 2023): 1.

ABOUT THE AUTHOR

Breannan Matris is a clairsentient and psychic medium who specializes in expelling ghosts. She grew up in a haunted house in the Chicago area where she had many encounters with a ghost she came to know as Elizabeth. Since that time, she has continued to have contact with ghosts and these experiences inspired her to delve into a study of the nature of ghosts. This endeavor has taken her down many paths.

In the 1980s, she was part of an Evergreen State College (Olympia Washington) research team that studied the near-death experience. A review of their findings was published in the peer-reviewed *Anabiosis–The Journal for Near-Death*,[23] parts of which were translated in nine European languages.

Breannan has worked as a psychic medium for California Psychics, a reputable psychic counseling service, and she has been a guest expert for the Portland (Oregon) Old Town Ghost Tour. She has been a guest speaker at the Oregon Ghost Conferences in Seaside and in Port Gamble, Oregon and a psychic with multiple ghost hunting groups. Breannan has also been a frequent guest on talk radio shows in the Pacific Northwest and Canada.

Currently, Breannan has a private practice clearing ghosts and is available to speak about her research on the near-death experience and encounters with the paranormal. Breannan is an ordained minister (Swami Achalanda) through the Temple of Kriya Yoga in Chicago.

www.ingramcontent.com/pod-product-compliance
Lightning Source LLC
LaVergne TN
LVHW041546070526
838199LV00046B/1844